PAUL WILLIAMSON

Secrets of SUCCESSFUL PRAYER

To order additional copies of this book, contact:
Xlibris
844-714-8691
www.Xlibris.com
Orders@Xlibris.com

ISBN: Softcover   978-1-6641-7653-9
         EBook   978-1-6641-7652-2

Print information available on the last page

Rev. date: 05/22/2021

Secrets of
SUCCESSFUL PRAYER

SECRETS OF SUCCESSFULPRAYER

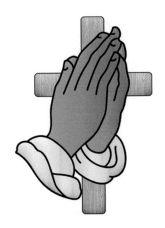

This little booklet you now hold in your hands, *Secrets of Successful Prayer*, provides answers to one simple question, a question many of us find ourselves asking whenever earthly troubles or pain press down on our thought: Why, even after we've opened our hearts to the power of God's love, do our prayers go unanswered?

Oftentimes, the reason prayers go unanswered is that we are trying to accomplish something that God does not want us to do. We also may not be doing something God specifically instructed us to do. We must pray to discover God's Will for us, and take on His Will for ourselves.

For example, consider the divorced couple with a ten year old son. The mother has custody. One day the son asks his father if he can come live with him, and his father agrees. When the father presents the idea to the mother, she thinks that it would be better to wait until the son is sixteen years old. The father disagrees and feels that the mother is being unreasonable. The parents argue their points, without resolution, then go their separate ways and begin to pray. Each prays that the other will see things from the other's point of view. The mother prays for the father to see that it would be better for the son to remain in her custody until he turns sixteen, and the father prays that the mother will allow the son to come live with him.

When we pray, however, we must seek to discover God's Will first, before we ask for our desires to be blessed. When we align our desires with God's Will, we can pray in confidence that our prayers will eventually be answered. Mary times prayers that seem to go unanswered are premature requests against God's Will.

Even seemingly bad circumstances turn out for the best when God's Will is at hand.

As in planting seed, once you have aligned your desires with God's will, day-to-day circumstances as well as your attitude must be watered with God's Word.

When Jesus' disciples asked how to pray, he gave them "The Lord's Prayer" (Luke 11). Every line in this prayer represents a truth or part of God's Will available to us as a foundation for our specific prayer requests.

As you read the Bible, you may find scriptures that address what you are personally experiencing. As you repeat and pray with these scriptures, God's promises will be revealed in your life and begin to make themselves manifest. An excellent scripture that can be used to water your prayers during the hard times is Psalm 23: "The Lord is my shepherd; I shall not want." This basic truth means that our Heavenly Father watches over His children, and He will answer our needs and wants according to his Will. "He makes me to lie down in green pastures" says that the Lord our shepherd knows our spiritual and physical needs, and He has the wisdom to help us meet these needs.

"Yea, though I walk through the valley of the shadow of death, I will fear no evil, for You are with me." The valleys and dark shadows of life often conceal danger or troubles and have the potential to create anxiety and fear of the unknown. However, as part of God's flock, we are protected. By trusting in God's covering and watchful attention, we can take comfort. He keeps us safe, and gives us the ability to make peace with our enemies.

"My cup runs over"; her David, the author, shows how God promises to grant us prosperity as we continue to keep ourselves in His care. Psalm 23 describes a foundation of security, peace and prosperity. Likewise, the Lord's Prayer provides a platform for honor, selflessness, obedience, prosperity, forgiveness, love, right standing, protection, and praise. These are the kind of principles that you should look for when choosing scriptures to water your prayers.

MAR 11:23 "I tell you the truth, if anyone says to this mountain, 'Go, throw yourself into the sea,' and does not doubt in his heart but believes that what he says will happen, it will be done for him.

MAR 11:24 Therefore I tell you, whatever you ask for in prayer, believe that you have received it, and it will be yours.

God's promise for prayer is simple; as Jesus said in Mark 11:23,24. Doubt is our enemy.

More than anything else, our hearts contain the answers to our prayers. We need to believe that the things that we ask for will happen – this is essential. But we also need to make those requests unselfishly.

1JO 3:21 Dear friends, if our hearts do not condemn us, we have confidence before God.

1JO 3:22 and receive from him anything we ask, because we obey his commands and do what pleases him.

JAM 4:3 When you ask, you do not receive, because you ask with wrong motives, that you may spend what you get on your pleasures.

Even though God already knows what our needs are before we ask, we still must ask His will and be specific in our requests. We also must realize that our schedules and timelines may differ from God's. Psalm 1:3 tells us that we must be 'like a tree' that bears fruit 'in its season' we cannot expect that God will answer our prayers if we ask Him today and turn to horoscopes or fortune tellers tomorrow. A season could be a day, week, moth, or longer, we have to exercise patience while avoiding the counsel of the ungodly.

Finally, there are some key things that we should come to believe through our experiences with prayer. The most important of these is that God gives us spiritual wisdom as we pray, so that we can learn to see God's purpose in our present circumstances.

ICO 2:9 However, as it is written: "No eye has seen, no ear has heard, no mind has conceived what God has prepared to those who love him."
ICO 2:10 but God has revealed it to us by his Spirit. The Spirit searches all things, even the deep things of God.
ICO 2:11 For among men knows the thoughts of a man except the man's spirit within him? In the same way no one knows the thoughts of God except the Spirit of God.
ICO 2:12 We have received the spirit of the world but the Spirit who is from God, that we may understand what God has freely given us.

Whenever we pray, we need to be aware of those around us because God may use those individuals to speak to us; His Spirit will lead us.

IJohn 5:14 affirms that if we ask 'according to His Will' our prayers will be answered successfully. These principles are secrets only to those who have not made the effort to seek them out. It is important for you to pray daily and use your Bible to confirm God's Will. As you share your new seeds for successful prayer, remember that Satan can only influence you through deception. In Luke 8:12, we are shown that the devil does not want us to believe or be saved. 'Satan comes immediately' to try and discourage us! But 2Tim 3:13-17 tells us that praying and using scriptures to water our seed equips us for any Godly thing that we set our hands to.

2TI 3:13 while evil men and impostors will go from bad to worse, deceiving and being deceived.

2TI 3:14 But as for you, continue in what you have learned and have become convinced of, because you know those from whom you learned it.

2TI 3:15 and how from infancy you have known the holy Scriptures, which are able to make you wise for salvation through faith in Christ Jesus.

2TI 3:16 All Scripture is God-breathed and is useful for teaching, rebuking, correcting and training in righteousness.

2TI 3:17 so that the man of God may be thoroughly equipped for every good work.

We sincerely hope that this message has blessed you. Thank you, and may the grace of God, the love of Christ, and the fellowship of the Holy Spirit be with you.

Thank you for ordering Secrets of Successful Prayer.
Successful prayer is the result of Christian principles and promises.
May you be BLESSED with the desires of your heart through prayer.
GOD BLESS

We welcome your comments!

Printed in the United States
by Baker & Taylor Publisher Services